This Way Up!

Access Routes into the Wicklow Mountains

David Herman

SHANKSMARE PUBLICATIONS

Layout by: Hot Pixels Design
Printed by: ColourBooks Ltd, Dublin 13
Published by: Shanksmare Publications, 41 Meadow Grove, Dublin 16

© David Herman 1997
First Published July 1997
ISBN 0 9514547 9 X
Cover: Fraughan Rock Glen (route SE 11). Photo by: Michael Costeloe

David Herman
The author has many years' hill walking experience in Wicklow.as well as other parts of Ireland and abroad. He lives in Dublin with his wife Mairin, herself an enthusiastic hill walker.

Other books written by the author under the Shanksmare imprint are: *Hill Strollers Wicklow* (new edition forthcoming), *Hill Walkers Kerry* (1997), *Hill Walkers Wicklow (1997)*, *Hill Walkers Connemara and Mayo* (1996), *Hill Walkers Donegal* (1995), and *North Leitrim Glens* (1993). Other books by the author include *Great Walks Ireland* (Ward Lock, 1991), *Walker's Companion* (Ward Lock, 1995), *Walking Ireland's Mountains* (Appletree, 1994). He is co-author of *Walk Guide East of Ireland* (Gill and Macmillan, 1996).

CONTENTS

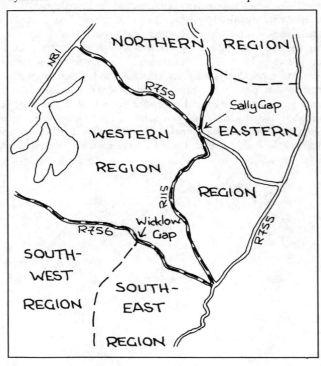

ACKNOWLEDGEMENTS

This book originated in a book entitled 'Dublin and Wicklow Mountains: Access Routes for the Hill Walker', first published by the Irish Ramblers Club in 1976, which ran to many printings and several editions.

The team who organised the production of the book were Jean Boydell, Michael Casey, Eithne Cassin-Kennedy and myself, David Herman. Of course, we four alone did not suggest or explore all the routes in the book - many members of the Club contributed in various ways. In particular, the late Margaret Casey drew the sketches (and sketch maps) for the original book, a few of which are reproduced here in her memory.

This book is an updated and expanded version of the original book, with modern layout and design, but many of the routes are the same or variations of those in the original book. It is thus a tribute to all the members of the Irish Ramblers Club who contributed to the original book in its various editions.

WHAT THIS BOOK IS ABOUT

As a hill walker you may have stood on a road in a mountain valley such as Glendalough and wondered how you were going to traverse the forests and steep ground between you and the uplands. In the Wicklow Mountains the uplands are generally easy to cross since they are mostly open though trackless country. It is the intermediate region between motor road and uplands which, as it consists all too often of forest, cliff, farmland or built-up area, is difficult to traverse. Yet there are paths and tracks across this intermediate region though they may be difficult to find and follow. These, together with a few footbridges and points where rivers may be forded, are described in the following pages.

A map alone is not sufficient to find all these routes. Some are not marked on the maps. Others are marked but not always correctly. Even those which are marked are much easier to follow if the map is supplemented by a few words of description. All the routes chosen lead into the mountain range proper (not into isolated peripheral hills) and so each route is the starting point for a full day's hill walking.

However access is not the only criterion. Parking possibilities are also taken into account: unless otherwise stated it is possible to park several cars (or more) at the start of each route. Attempts have been made (not always successfully) to devise routes which are attractive in themselves. Details have not, in general, been given of how to find your way *off* the mountains and back onto the road. For two reasons. Firstly it is easier to find your way down as the route ahead is generally clearer than when walking uphill. Secondly the sketch maps, simple though they are, give some idea of the route, though it has to be said that text is almost impossible to interpret when used to describe the route in the opposite direction to that intended. Of course it is advisable to walk the route uphill before attempting it in the opposite direction.

No attempt has been made to provide specific routes through the uplands: that is left to your inventiveness, particular interests and other guidebooks. However a concise but comprehensive description of the mountains is included - its terrain, views and special attractions - which will enable you to choose routes you will enjoy walking.

The Sketch Maps: The sketch maps given in this book are conventionally oriented, that is north towards the top, but are not drawn to scale.

Symbols used in the Sketch Maps: The symbols used on the sketch maps are shown on page 64. Symbols are omitted where not relevant.

Grid References: These four or six digit numbers, generally printed in brackets after some locations in the text (particularly the start of each access route) are used to pinpoint places on the map. The system is explained on OS maps.

Abbreviations in the Route Descriptions: These are L and R for left and right and N, S, E and W for the four cardinal directions.

Distances in the Route Descriptions: Metric units are used throughout, except where a car is implied. In these cases miles are used. The mile figures are to the appropriate degree of precision. On some car journeys to the start of routes the term 'zero miles' after a location means the point from which all subsequent cumulative distances are taken. They are also indicated where possible on the sketch maps.

MAPS

The best maps for walkers are the Ordnance Survey 1:50 000 sheets 50, which covers the mountains near Dublin, 56 which covers nearly all the mountain area and 62 which covers its south. Unfortunately, the 1:50 000 maps are particularly bad in depicting tracks and forests, two of the most important features to get right for access routes.

The OS half-inch to the mile sheet 16 covers the entire mountain area and much more besides, but the scale is far too small. The 1:25 000 Glendalough map, issued by the National Parks and Wildlife Service (NWPS), covers only a small area but is extremely comprehensive in its depiction of track and paths. It is available in the NPWS outlets in Glendalough.

TRANSPORT BY BUS

The following Dublin Bus services (☎ 01-873 4222) may be useful.

For the north-west corner of the mountains note 47 (**Tibradden**, infrequent), 47A (**Rockbrook**, infrequent), 47B (**Grange Road**, moderately frequent), 49A (**Bohernabreena**, fairly frequent though there is virtually no Sunday service).

For the north-east corner note 44 (**Enniskerry**, frequent), 44B (**Barnacullia, Glencullen**, infrequent), 185 (**Shop River**, about 2.5km west of Enniskerry, moderately frequent) and 145 from Bray to **Kilmacanoge** (infrequent).

For the west (N81) note 65 to **Blessington** (frequent), **Ballymore Eustace** and **Ballyknockan** (both very infrequent).

There is a very useful service along the east of the range terminating in **Glendalough**. This is the St Kevin's Bus (☎ 01-281 8119) which runs from St Stephen's Green in Dublin through **Kilmacanoge**, **Roundwood** and **Laragh** to Glendalough. The service is fairly infrequent.

Reid's Buses (☎ 0404-67671) runs a regular service between Wicklow town and Glendalough.

There are two Irish Bus / Bus Eireann local services (ie buses which stop anywhere as long as it is safe to do so) which might be useful for hill walkers. They are bus timetable 132 (very infrequent) which runs from Dublin along the N81 on the west of the range with a useful stop at **Annalecky Cross** near Donard, and timetable 133 (frequent) which runs along the N11 (with diversions to villages) on the east of the range.

There is only one Irish Bus / Bus Eireann express (ie limited stop) service which might be useful for hill walkers. It is given on bus timetable 5 with variations which traverse each side of the mountains from Dublin. That on the west stops at **Blessington** and at **Annalecky Cross**. That on the east stops at **Bray** and **Ashford** (GR 2797).

TRANSPORT BY CAR

I must first apologise for assuming both here and in the paragraph 'Approach' in the route descriptions that you are travelling from Dublin. I can only plead that this is the most likely assumption and any other would be unduly wordy.

Getting to the mountain area from Dublin is not easy mainly because of inadequate sign-posting. The method used here is to use 'jumping-off' points. For each route first drive from Dublin to the appropriate jumping-off point (indicated by underlining in the paragraph 'Approach'). From there drive to the starting point as indicated in that paragraph.

Here are the jumping-off points (the figure in brackets given after each jumping-off point represents miles from central Dublin):

Blessington (18): Drive through Harold's Cross, Terenure and Temple-ogue following signs for the N81.

Donard (31) (grid ref 9397): Follow signs for the N81, turning left at the 'Olde Tollhouse', about 11 miles beyond Blessington.

Drumgoff crossroads, Glenmalure (36) (grid ref 1090): Drive to Laragh (see below), continue on R755 for about 1 mile. Fork right (signposted Glenmalure) for Drumgoff crossroads, which is about 4½ miles further on.

Enniskerry (13): Follow signs for Ranelagh and Dundrum, then continue straight ahead.

Glenasmole (9) (grid ref 0922): Follow signs for the N81, taking the first exit at the roundabout which leads onto the M50. Turn right at the nearby tee onto the R114 and continue straight ahead for 3.7 miles, turning left here into Glenasmole (no signpost). (Note: there may well be changes in the road system at the M50 roundabout in the near future.)

Glencullen crossroads (11) (grid ref 1820): Follow signs for Ranelagh and Dundrum, turn right (signposted) off the Enniskerry road at Ste-paside or Kiltiernan. Alternatively: Drive to Rockbrook (see below), turn left off the main road about 1 mile south of the village.

Glendalough (31): Follow signs for the M11/N11 initially through Lee-son Street and Donnybrook, turning right onto the R755 at Kilmacanoge.

Kilmacanoge (17) (grid ref 2414): Follow signs for the M11/N11.

Laragh (30) (grid ref 1496): Follow signs for the M11/N11, turning right onto the R755 at Kilmacanoge.

Rockbrook (6) (grid ref 1324): Follow signs for Rathfarnham, pass Rath-farnham Castle (on left), turn right shortly at Yellow House pub (on right). Continue straight ahead for about 2½ miles. The village it is not signposted.

Roundwood (26): Follow signs for the M11/N11, turning right onto the R755 at Kilmacanoge.

Sally Gap (17) (grid ref 1311), Military Road: Drive initially through Harold's Cross and Terenure following signs for Rathfarnham. Pass Rathfarnham Castle on left, turn right shortly at Yellow House pub (on right). Turn right onto Scholarstown Road 1.2 miles from the pub and second left almost immediately onto Stocking Lane. Continue straight

8

ahead to Killakee carpark, where you should veer right uphill, thus heading for the Military Road and Sally Gap.

Parking in the Wicklow Mountains: If you are in a large party with many cars you should, as well as trying to minimise the number of cars you use, try to park in carparks rather than along the margins of roads, at forestry entrances etc. This applies especially in fine weather in summer. The following large carparks, listed roughly from north-west to south-east are particularly suited to large groups. Carparks marked with an asterisk are comparatively small.

Cruagh Wood (grid ref 1222), Pine Forest Wood (1322), Crone (1914), Djouce Woods (three carparks south of 2113)), Kippure Wood* (0714), Ballynultagh Gap* (0410), Military Road south of Sally Gap (1308), Ballinastoe Wood* (1907), Sally Gap Road near Lough Tay (1607), near Ballyknockan* (0107), Wicklow Gap (0700), Glenmacnass (1102), Glendalough at the Visitor Centre and at the Upper Lake (1296, 1196), Baravore (0694).

A Word of Caution to Car Travellers: There have been many thefts in recent years from cars parked in remote mountain locations. It is therefore advisable to hide valuables in unattended cars, or better still not to leave any valuables in them at all.

SAFETY

The object of this book is to get you into open mountain country and to help to get you out again. It is of little help in finding your way around the mountains. The following guidelines are the basic minimum to allow you to venture safely into the mountains:

- Wear and carry proper equipment. Walking boots that give ankle support are essential. Always carry raingear, food, a whistle and a map and compass. Know how to use the map and compass!

- Do not press on regardless. In bad or deteriorating conditions turn back, or head for lower ground. If you think you can just about make it, don't try.

- Do not go hill walking alone. Four is the minimum number for safety. This allow one to remain with a person who might be injured and two to seek help.

- Remember that landmarks may have changed between the time these routes were explored and the time you walk them. In particular, there may be new stiles and forest tracks, forest may have been cleared and the Wicklow Way may have been re-routed; keep all this in mind (as well as the possibility that the author may have erred!) if the route does not make sense.
- Do not enter forested areas if you are not quite sure how you are going to emerge. You may easily be disoriented among the trees or find your way blocked by closely spaced, mature trees.
- Take care when attempting to cross mountain streams. During and after rain, mountain streams swell rapidly, so it may be impossible to cross a stream which you had easily crossed a few hours previously. If you cannot cross it is usually better to try upstream.
- Leave a clear message at base of where you are going and when you intend to be back.
- Get a forecast before you set out. You can get a forecast for the Dublin area by ringing 1550 123 814.
- If the worst happens you can summon help by ringing 999.

THE COUNTRY CODE

Please obey the Country Code and respect the life of the countryside on your walks. In particular:
- Don't take dogs into sheep rearing country, that is virtually the entire mountain area, especially during the lambing season.
- Don't stand on fence wires. They may look the same afterwards but will have been irretrievably damaged.
- If it is necessary to climb gates do so at the hinged end.
- Keep to zig-zags on steep ascents and descents.
- If there are specially constructed paths on or near your route keep to them.
- Litter: DON'T. To go further: it would be a great service to those walking after you if walkers would pick up litter left by others. After all, litter cannot remove itself and the local authorities cannot remove it in remote areas.

- Don't widen paths by walking on their edges. Either walk in the centre of the path (preferably) or well away from it. If possible avoid eroded paths during or after wet weather. This is particularly important in the Djouce area, on the Spink south of the Upper Lake in Glendalough and in some areas near Dublin where footpath erosion is widespread. Access routes leading to eroded paths are noted in the text.

RIGHTS OF WAY

Except in State forests, in the Wicklow Mountains National Park and on the Wicklow Way you have no absolute right to be anywhere in the mountains. Especially near Dublin, farmers are understandably worried by the frequent vandalism with which they are faced. It is hard for them to distinguish between polite walkers and destructive yobbos, so they may end up by trying to keep out *all* trespassers. In these circumstances I am glad to pay tribute to those landowners, particularly the Guinness family of Lough Tay, who have been more than generous in facilitating walkers. I hope hill walkers will never betray their trust by bad behaviour.

One would have thought that with the passing of the Occupiers' Liability Act 1995, which removes any remaining doubt that landowners have responsibility for accidents that occur on their land, there would be a more relaxed attitude to walkers. Not so. The Act has resulted in unfriendly signs ending with the words UNAUTHORISED ENTRY IS PROHIBITED. However, the good news is that the representatives of the ICMSA, the organisation behind these signs have declared that they are not intended to prevent access for walkers. So that's all right then - unless you are unused to our strange ways and do not realise that signs can mean the exact opposite of what they declare.

Given this totally unsatisfactory state of affairs it is prudent to interpret signs rather than simply obey them. In these routes I have not knowingly led you into areas in which confrontations are likely, but no one knows where disputes may flare in the future.

If you would like to preserve access routes in Wicklow and throughout the country the organisation to contact is 'Keep Ireland Open' (☎ 493 4239).

NORTHERN REGION

This region is bounded on the south by the road running west from Sally Gap, by the Military Road and by Glencree.

General Access Difficulties

On the north the foothills of the Dublin Mountains rise from the suburbs of the city itself. The access problems in the area nearer Dublin, particularly on the north and east of the mountains, are simple: how to

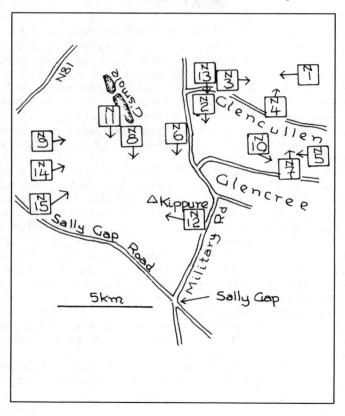

penetrate the urban sprawl and farms and, surprisingly the considerable stretches of forest barring the hills beyond. Further west and south the problems are less severe as this area is less built-up, though farm and forest can still cause difficulties. Access from the Sally Gap Road northwards is poor, as there is much forestry and a large turf-cutting operation in the area. The more southerly stretch of the Military Road in this region offers easy access both east and west.

Terrain

West of Glenasmole lies a broad range of peaks stretching south from Slievenabawnoge to Seefin (621m). The terrain is good towards the north with scattered gorse bushes and short heather. The lower ground between Corrig and Seefingan (724m) is markedly less good, with many wet and boggy places; the line of boundary stones along this stretch, marking the boundary between Dublin and Wicklow, is a useful navigational aid. Views along this stretch are excellent for the area. Seefingan and Seefin at the south-west end of the ridge are crowned by enormous passage graves.

East of Seefingan a bleak, wet, exposed ridge extends to Kippure, the end nearer Kippure being especially bad. Kippure at 757m is the highest point in Co Dublin. Its only distinguishing feature - it doesn't need another! - is the TV mast on its summit; otherwise it is a characterless boggy mound. The area south and east of it towards the Sally Gap Road (R759) and the Military Road is equally dull. Northwards stretches the heathery valley of upper Glenasmole with its numerous turf cuttings. However the area round Kippure is not without redeeming features: etched into the eastern slopes of these mountains are the secluded and beautiful corrie lakes of the Lough Brays.

The main features east of the Military Road are the two similar glacial valleys of Glencullen and Glencree. The area north of Glencullen, which borders directly on the city and whose atmosphere is dominated by it, is a dry bumpy plateau of heather and occasional gorse, along with heavily eroded paths. In spite of its unpromising location this is a pleasant enough area commanding wide views of the city and beyond.

A broad ridge between the two valleys stretching from Cruagh to Prince William's Seat (555m) has a slightly more remote air, with long, fairly good views. The terrain is coarse grass and short heather but it is fairly wet particularly towards the west.

13

ROUTE N1: BARNACULLIA TO THREE ROCK MOUNTAIN

Road and track to start, followed by an initially intermittent path through ferns and gorse with good close-up views over Dublin.

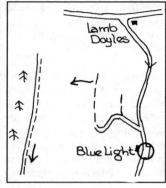

Approach: At Lamb Doyles Pub (174252), situated at the junctions of Blackglen, Harold's Grange and Woodside Roads take Woodside Road for 1 mile. Park in the carpark opposite the Blue Light Pub (181242).   Buses 44B (to Barnacullia), 47, 47A, 47B.

Route: Walk a few metres back towards Dublin, take the first road L, fork shortly L uphill and continue past quarry workings on what is now a grassy track traversing open country. Where the track shortly reaches level ground, take any of a maze of paths L to head roughly W to forest. At the forest turn L onto a path for Three Rock.

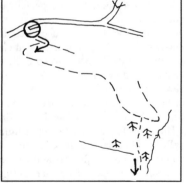

ROUTE N2: CRUAGH WOOD CARPARK TO CRUAGH

Forest tracks and paths on a route which ends on moorland close to the cairn marking Cruagh.

Approach: Drive through Rockbrook, veer R over 1 mile S. Park shortly in the large carpark on the L (127226). Buses 47, 47A.

Route: Take the forest track from the carpark, turning first R onto another track. Where this track levels shortly before a hairpin bend take a clear path on the R to emerge at a narrow line of trees at about 139217 on the E side of the Cruagh spur.

Note: if coming in the opposite direction look out for the narrow line of trees at the R end of a block of forest and follow the path to its L.

ROUTE N3: PINE FOREST CARPARK TO FAIRY CASTLE

A walk partly through forest ends on a track on the Tibradden spur.

Approach: Drive through <u>Rockbrook</u>, turn L at the tee about 1 mile S to park in the nearby carpark (139226). Bus 47A to Rockbrook, otherwise 47, 47B. If coming by bus you can take a short-cut to the carpark.

Route: Note that though short cuts look tempting, there are many paths in this area and it is easy to get lost.

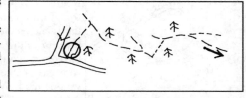

Cross the bar at the end of the carpark, follow the track beyond and turn R at the tee. Continue straight ahead to reach the end of the track at a small disused quarry. Here take a path steeply uphill (not the deeply rutted track). It ends at a track; continue upwards on it. Fork R shortly to keep on the crest of the Tibradden spur. Fairy Castle lies to the E.

ROUTE N4: GLENCULLEN TO FAIRY CASTLE

Not enjoyable, but the only feasible route to the Tibradden - Fairy Castle area from Glencullen (except for the Wicklow Way 1.5km to the W).

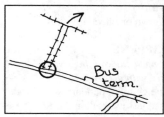

Approach: From <u>Glencullen crossroads</u> drive W, that is towards the head of the valley. Park in the area of the bus terminus on the R about 1 mile further on (parking is difficult hereabouts) (172208). Bus 44B.

Route: Walk about 100m W from the bus terminus, turning R here between two closely spaced fences. Walk upward (wet underfoot) to reach nearby open country with Fairy Castle to the N.

Note that this route is usually used to cross Glencullen, S to N. It is difficult to find if walking in the opposite direction.

ROUTE N5: GLENCULLEN TO PRINCE WILLIAM'S SEAT

A pleasant walk, mostly on a narrow path, with good views except through forest.

Approach: Drive S from <u>Glencullen crossroads</u> for 1.5 miles turning R here onto a narrow road (198189). It is possible to park carefully at some places along this road. Bus 44B.

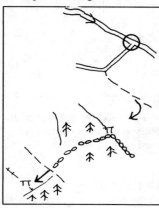

Route: Walk the road to the nearby tee. Turn L to take a track as far as the third field on the L. Turn R here off the track to follow an intermittent path to the corner of a thick wall (a stile at this corner is visible from afar). Keep the wall on the L to walk uphill into forest, down to a shallow valley and uphill again to cross a forest track. Continue straight ahead, mature forest on the L, to cross a stile. From here Raven's Rock is nearby to the SW and Prince William's Seat to its W.

Note 1: The path from Prince William's Seat to Knocknagun is badly eroded. Use this area only when necessary and take great care to minimise further damage. See also the Country Code (p.10).

Note 2: The road initially walked is not shown on sheet 56.

ROUTE N6: MILITARY ROAD TO KIPPURE

A slog through bogland and heather along a narrow bogcutters' road which is unfortunately edged here and there with debris.

Approach: Take the <u>Military Road</u> to the county boundary with Wicklow (signposted) (131196), where there is a narrow road on the R. There is some parking hereabouts.

Route: Walk along the narrow road (it is also possible to drive). The road ends after 2km or so but an intermittent path continues towards Kippure.

ROUTE N7: GLENCREE TO PRINCE WILLIAM'S SEAT

A walk mostly through forest to near the summit of Prince William's Seat.

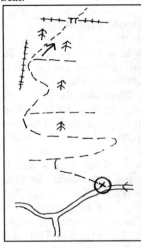

Approach: Drive to <u>Enniskerry</u>, turning R in the village centre to drive along the N side of Glencree. Park at the forest entrance on the R 2.9 miles from Enniskerry, where there is ample parking (185168). Bus 185.

Route: (This is the present (1997) route of the Wicklow Way.) Take the forest track to turn R at a nearby tee, ignore a track on the R, fork L at the forest edge onto a narrow path through trees. Emerging from the trees cross one stile. The rounded summit of Prince William's Seat lies nearby to the NW but is out of sight.

Note: The path from Prince William's Seat to Knocknagun is badly eroded. Use this area only when necessary and take great care to minimise further damage. See also the Country Code (p.10).

ROUTE N8: GLENASMOLE TO KIPPURE

A gentle uphill on an old track, with lovely deciduous trees alongside to start, soon degenerates a little into a walk over moorland, still on the track.

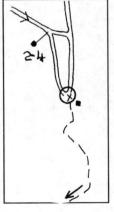

Approach: Turn L into <u>Glenasmole</u> (zero miles), fork R (2.4 miles), park at or before the hairpin bend to the L at 2.8 miles (109199). Since considerate parking is severely limited at this bend, it may be advisable to park along the narrow road before it.

Route: Cross the gate at the hairpin bend and follow the wide track beyond. After about 2.5km (at about 119183) the track bends sharp R and starts to descend. Kippure lies S.

Note: The track extends much further than shown on the current edition of sheet 56.

ROUTE N9: BALLYMOREFINN HILL FROM THE WEST

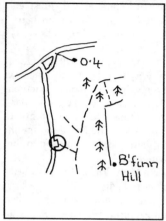

A not so attractive route through forest and clear-felled areas gives access to Ballymorefinn Hill and thence on a long gentle uphill to Seahan.

Approach: Drive past the turn L to <u>Glenasmole</u> (zero miles), fork L onto a minor road at 0.4 miles, park in the forest entrance on the L at 1.7 miles (076207).

Route: Take the forest track to turn L at the nearby tee, walk onward for over 1km (15 mins) to take a clear but muddy path on the R through trees. Shortly emerge from forest at about 084219 with Ballymorefinn Hill and Seahan to the S.

ROUTE N10: GLENCULLEN TO PRINCE WILLIAM'S SEAT, KNOCKNAGUN

Clear-felled forest forms a not very attractive foreground to pleasant views over Glencullen.

Approach from W: Drive through <u>Rockbrook</u>, turn L at the tee over 1 mile S of the village, pass the layby for the bus terminus on the L about 2.5 miles further on and take the next turn R, Boranaralty Lane. Drive to the nearby bridge around which there is limited parking (169205).

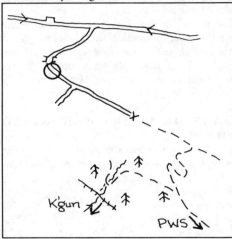

Approach from E: Drive W (that is, towards the head of the valley) from <u>Glencullen Cross-roads</u>, turning L into Boranaralty Lane after about a mile. Drive to the nearby bridge.

Route: Nearly all of this route follows the present (1997) line of the Wicklow Way. Continue onward from the bridge, ignoring the nearby R turn to follow a narrow road steadily uphill SE. At the first gate it narrows to a track and less than 10 mins beyond this, turn R onto another track running steeply uphill to meet a tee. To reach Prince William's Seat turn L into forest, still on a track, and SW on emerging from it. To reach Knocknagun turn R, still on a track, to reach a stream with a rough path running upward along its side. Take this path to reach nearby open ground (168196). Knocknagun lies SW.

Note: The path from Prince William's Seat to Knocknagun is badly eroded. Use this area only when necessary and take great care to minimise further damage. See also the Country Code (p.10).

19

ROUTE N11: GLENASMOLE TO CORRIG

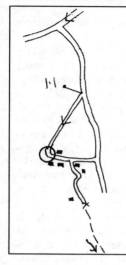

An old meandering track through abandoned fields with good views of Glenasmole Reservoir.

Approach: Turn L into <u>Glenasmole</u> (zero miles), fork R onto a side road (the first) at 1.1 miles, park at a right angle bend at 1.6 miles (096210). There is limited space for careful parking on the verge along here and at the start of the route proper.

Route: Walk downhill from the right angle bend, turning R into the nearby laneway. At its end pass through a gate and take the track beyond into open land. The track contours SE before petering out after over 1km. From here Corrig lies to the SW.

ROUTE N12: UPPER LOUGH BRAY TO KIPPURE

A rather wet path gives good views from steep ground overlooking Upper Lough Bray, with Kippure within easy reach.

Approach: Take the <u>Military Road</u> past the acute turn for Enniskerry on the L (at grid ref 1417). About 1.6 miles further on park at a quarry on the L (143152).

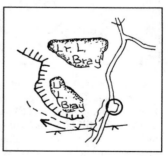

Route: Turn L out of the carpark and walk about 100m to where an electricity line crosses the road. At about the first pole on the R, take a narrow path on this side to cross a stream. Continue on what becomes a wide, wet path running along the top of high ground overlooking Upper Lough Bray. Kippure lies to the W reached (eventually) by the TV road.

ROUTE N13: PINE FOREST TO CRUAGH

A low starting point, but one convenient to buses, leads to a walk mostly on track through forest which gives access to the mountains between Glencullen and Glencree.

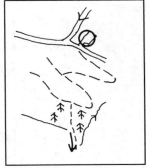

Approach: Drive through <u>Rockbrook</u>, turn L at the tee more than 1 mile S to park in the nearby large carpark (139227). Bus 47A to Rockbrook, otherwise 47, 47B. If walking from Rockbrook you can take an obvious short-cut to the carpark.

Route: Cross the road from the carpark, take the track here to a tee, turn L and walk round one hairpin bend. Just after take the clear path on the L upward through forest to emerge at a line of trees at about 139217 on the E side of the Cruagh spur.

Note: if coming from the opposite direction look out for a narrow fringe of trees running S and follow the path to its L. This fringe is at the R end of a block of forest and has a stream to its R.

ROUTE N14: SEAHAN FROM THE WEST

A high starting point (490m) gives a walk mostly through forest, initially on track and path, ending with a short but muddy section high on the shoulder of Seahan.

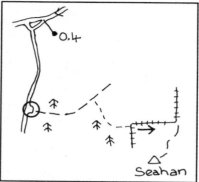

Approach: Drive past the junction L to <u>Glenasmole</u> (zero miles), fork L onto a minor road at 0.4 miles, park in the forest entrance on the L at 2.1 miles (073201).

Route: Walk the forest track for less than 10 mins to where mature forest ends. Take the path on the R here to reach a clear firebreak and follow it to the corner of a fence. Walk straight ahead following the fence to a track running R to the nearby summit of Seahan.

ROUTE N15: NEAR ATHDOWN TO SEEFIN

A short walk on a forest track is prelude to a steady climb to near the summit of Seefin giving quite good views.

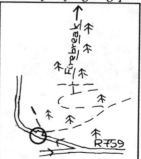

Approach: Take the N81 towards (not to) <u>Blessington</u>, turning L onto the R759. Follow the signs for Sally Gap for 5.6 miles, here taking an acute turn L. (If you have driven as far as the entrance to Kippure Woods, you have gone a little too far.) Drive 0.7 miles to the first forest entrance on the R (068144).

Route: Take the forest track on the R (E). After about 10 mins, walk round the first hairpin bend, a L (here ignore the rough track running NE). Shortly after turn L steeply uphill to immediately cross a narrow track. Continue upward on a firebreak until it ends above forest at about 075159, with the summit of Seefin nearby to N.

EASTERN REGION

This region is bounded on the north by Glencree and on the west by the Military Road (R115).

General Access Problems

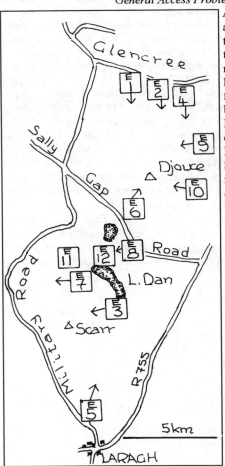

Access is possible virtually anywhere eastward from the Military Road. From the north and east access is more difficult because of long stretches of forest and farmland in Glencree and bordering the Enniskerry - Roundwood road and its extension south to Laragh. However access from the Sally Gap Road (R759) north-eastwards is much easier, though even here there are some stretches of forest.

Terrain

South of heavily wooded Glencree is a broad spur. At its west is the mass of the Tonduffs (642m), a rather boggy, featureless area bordering the Liffey Head Bog. Eastward at about grid ref 1713 lies the Raven's Glen where slabby rocks may cause a slippery descent from the Tonduffs in wet conditions. East of the Tonduffs lies Maulin, a well-shaped cone with a drier covering of heather, beyond which the spur terminates abruptly at Deerpark. This beautiful wooded amphitheatre is backed by Powerscourt Waterfall, the highest in Ireland.

South of Glensoulan, the upper valley of the Dargle, War Hill is an unimpressive outlier of the much more memorable Djouce (725m). Unfortunately, Djouce's eastern side has heavily eroded paths and so special care should be taken in this area to avoid further damage. A south-running spur carries a line of posts and the Wicklow Way, both useful aids to navigation. This spur ends to the south with magnificent views over Lough Tay.

The area viewed from this spur, the mountains of Fancy (595m), Knocknacloghoge (534m) and Scarr (641m) and the valleys between them, form probably the finest mountain landscape in Wicklow. Though its summit is mundane, Fancy's setting is extremely impressive, with its eastern side dropping in mighty cliffs to heart-shaped Lough Tay. Knocknacloghoge's and particularly Scarr's summit are more impressive, though they lack Fancy's rugged flank. The northern spur of Scarr is the complicated hummocky tangle of Kanturk Mountain, overlooking the tranquil and comparatively large Lough Dan.

West of the entire line of mountains stretching from Maulin to Scarr and reaching beyond this section across the Military Road is a gently sloping and rather featureless region of bogland. This is an area of distant peaks and wide horizons. Not an area from which to emerge with dry feet!

ROUTE E1: GLENCREE TO TONDUFFS

A short stretch through forest, then along the edge of the crag-bound Raven's Glen on an increasingly rough path through high heather.

Approach from the W: Drive the <u>Military Road</u>, turning L onto the road which runs along S side of Glencree (signposted Glencree Drive). Continue for 3.0 miles, parking at the small layby on the R (179146). (Note: there is parking here for only 4-5 cars, so see note below.)

Approach from Enniskerry: Drive S from <u>Enniskerry</u> on the Round-wood road (signposted). About 2 miles further on turn R (signposted Glencree). Pass the prominent Powerscourt Gates and the large carpark at Crone. Park in the layby on the L about 1 mile beyond the carpark (179146).

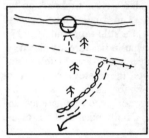

Route: Take the path at the layby, cross the nearby stile and climb to a forest track. Turn L and follow the track for a few minutes to a broad wall on the R. Cross the fence here at the break just beyond the corner of the wall and follow it upwards on a path through high heather and rocks, the wall close on the R, until the wall swings NW. The Tonduffs lie to the W on an intermittent path.

Note: This route may also be easily reached from Crone carpark (192142) 1km away, by taking the forest track from the carpark, and ignoring one forest track joining it acutely on the L. The corner of the wall, before which you turn L, should be easily visible from this direction.

ROUTE E2: GLENCREE TO MAULIN

A short forest walk on the level is followed by a steep climb through trees with widening views. The route ends on the eastern shoulder of Maulin.

Approach: Drive S from <u>Enniskerry</u> on the Roundwood road (signposted). About 2 miles further on turn R (signposted Glencree). Pass the prominent Powerscourt Gates and park in the large carpark at Crone (192142), about 1 mile beyond.

Route: Pass the bar at the end of the carpark, turn immediately L onto a path. Cross one forest track to reach a second at a Wicklow Way signpost. Turn L onto this track. Pass a narrow path on the R (it is flanked by a stream) and a few minutes later, take a clear firebreak on the R directly upward. Cross one forest track to reach open country at a stile (at about 195127). The E shoulder of Maulin lies directly ahead.

If using this route for the descent follow the stone wall NE over the eastern shoulder of Maulin, then follow for about 100m another wall heading W, here descend to a gate leading into forest (there is a holly bush to the L of the gate).

Note: Paths on this shoulder of Maulin and beyond towards the Tonduffs are eroded. Use this area only when necessary and take great care to minimise further damage. See also the Country Code (p.10).

ROUTE E3: LOUGH DAN TO SCARR

A track offers gradually widening views over Lough Dan, especially good where the route ends on a shoulder of Scarr.

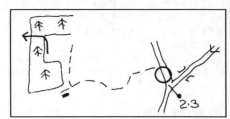

Approach: Drive to Roundwood, turn R here (signposted Lough Dan), turn R after 2.3 miles (still following signs for Lough Dan) and park close by on waste ground on the L (158017). Bus: St Kevin's.

Route: Walk onward towards Lough Dan, shortly taking the first track L. Still on this track walk along one side of a block of forest, but where the track leaves the forest edge, turn L to follow the forest along two sides, then turn L through a wide firebreak. At its end at 146023, Scarr lies to the W, reached on a rough path.

Note: If coming in the opposite direction, walk to the corner of forest on the NE spur of Scarr, take the wide firebreak near this corner.

ROUTE E4: GLENCREE TO DJOUCE, MAULIN

Increasingly dull forest ends high above the majestic Deerpark, a partly wooded bowl terminated by cliffs over which the waters of Powerscourt Waterfall tumble.

Approach: : Drive S from Enniskerry on the Roundwood road (signposted). About 2 miles further on turn R (signposted Glencree). Pass the prominent Powerscourt Gates and park in the large carpark at Crone (192142), about 1 mile further on.

Route: Pass the bar at the end of the carpark, turn immediately L

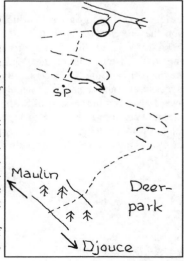

onto a path. Cross one forest track to reach a second at a Wicklow Way signpost (the rest of the route is on the present (1997) route of the Wicklow Way). Turn L here and walk the track upwards through forest. Ignore one minor track L to reach open ground above the Deerpark. Continue on a path overlooking Deerpark on the L to cross a band of trees and emerge from forest at 192122. Follow the Wicklow Way L for Djouce and the forest edge R for Maulin.

Note: Paths on this side of Djouce are heavily eroded. Use this area only when necessary and take great care to minimise further damage. See also the Country Code (p.10).

ROUTE E5: NEAR LARAGH TO SCARR

A pleasant walk through open forest and high pastures with excellent, wide views.

Approach: Drive to <u>Laragh</u>, turn R onto the Military Road here (signposted Sally Gap). Drive for 0.6 miles, parking at the forest entrance on the R (140976). Bus: St Kevin's.

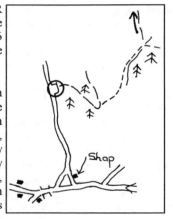

Route: Take the forest track, which is on the present (1997) route of the Wicklow Way, to the first hairpin bend, a L. Here, still on the Way, take the path heading R, which shortly leaves forest and continues steeply upward. Now on the S spur of Scarr, continue generally N keeping to high ground on a rough track, which runs part of the way towards the mountain.

ROUTE E6: SALLY GAP ROAD TO WHITE HILL, DJOUCE

An exceptionally high start (460m) in scenic surroundings, and a short forest walk which ends in open country high on White Hill.

Approach: Drive to <u>Kilmacanoge</u>, turning R here onto the R755. Continue straight ahead for about 7 miles, turning R here (signposted Sally Gap) onto the R759. Drive straight ahead for a further 2.1 miles, to pass the large gate pillars on the L ('Pier Gates'). Shortly after pass a small carpark on the R. Park just beyond here in a larger carpark on the same side (169074).

Route: The entire route is on the present (1997) line of the Wicklow Way. Take the forest track, turn L at the nearby first crossroads, fork shortly L, ignore a rough track on the R on emerging from forest, turn shortly R uphill to reach the JB Malone memorial on the SW spur of White Hill.

Note: Paths on this side of Djouce are heavily eroded. Use this area only when necessary and take great care to minimise further damage. See also the Country Code (p.10).

ROUTE E7: LOUGH DAN TO INCHAVORE RIVER

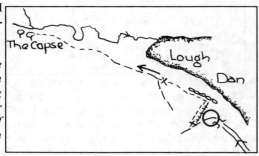

A lovely gentle walk, initially above the shores of Lough Dan and then along the Inchavore River to end at a copse of deciduous trees with Knocknacloghoge and Kanturk within reach.

Approach: Drive to <u>Roundwood</u>, turn R for Lough Dan (signposted) and follow signs for Lough Dan to park at the end of tarmac, where the road crosses a bridge (149030). Park considerately. Bus: St Kevin's.

29

Route: Walk uphill along the track (an extension of the road), shortly turning R through a narrow gate, the first. Take the path beyond which ends at a track. Turn R here and take it to its end. Continue through fields parallel to the Inchavore River to the prominent copse at 133046 with Knocknacloghoge to the NE and Kanturk to the SW.

Note: See also route E11 for directions from the copse to Kanturk.

ROUTE E8: PIER GATES TO KNOCKNACLOGHOGE, FANCY

A lovely walk, initially steeply downhill, on narrow road and track in the midst of some of the finest scenery in Wicklow.

Approach: Drive to <u>Kilmacanoge</u>, turning R here onto the R755. Turn R after about 7 miles (signposted Sally Gap) onto the R759. Drive uphill for 2.0 miles, to pass a gate on the L. Park shortly near the large gate pillars on that side ('Pier Gates') (173065). Bus: St Kevin's.

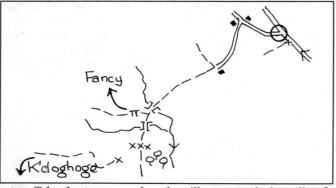

Route: Take the tarmac road at the pillars to reach the valley floor. Walk onward on a track to cross a wide bridge. Turn immediately R over a stile and onto another track. Turn R off it shortly to climb to Fancy to the NW. For Knocknacloghoge, keep on the initial track to cross another bridge. Immediately take the R-most of three gates, walk up through a field, cross the gate at its top, take the track beyond which runs along the N side of the mountain. Leave it after about 30 mins to climb Knocknacloghoge to the S.

ROUTE E9: DJOUCE WOODS TO DJOUCE

A short stretch of forest is followed by a steady upward march with gradually widening views.

Approach: Drive S from <u>Enniskerry</u> on the Round-wood road (signposted). Turn R off the main road 2.2 miles beyond Enniskerry (signposted Roundwood). Park in the third forest carpark on the R along this road (210113). Bus: St Kevin's.

Route: Take the path at the S end of the carpark, follow it across a nearby narrow stream and open ground. Walk W to re-enter forest for a short distance and where convenient cross a fence L to take a firebreak upwards, forest on the R. At the crest of the hill at 195114 meet the Wicklow Way with Djouce to SW.

Note: Paths on this side of Djouce are heavily eroded. Use this area only when necessary and take great care to minimise further damage. See also the Country Code (p.10). In particular, do not walk the eroded direct path to Djouce. Instead follow the Wicklow Way to the crest of the White Hill-Djouce ridge.

ROUTE E10: WHITE HILL, DJOUCE FROM THE EAST

Forest tracks to start, then a long upward slog with only gradually widening views ends on the magnificent S spur of Djouce.

Approach: Turn R at <u>Kilmacanoge</u> onto the R755 (zero miles). Continue straight ahead for 4.8 miles, turning R here onto a side road. Continue to a tee, turn L and park in nearby Ballinastoe Carpark on the R (194077). Bus: St Kevin's.

Route: Turn R out of the carpark onto a forest track and R again immediately. Turn L to follow initially an electricity line. Where it swings L walk straight uphill, forest on the L. At the crest of the hill turn R onto

the Wicklow Way with White Hill and Djouce ahead.
Note: Paths on this side of Djouce are heavily eroded. Use this area only when necessary and take great care to minimise further damage. See also the Country Code (p.10).

ROUTE E11: CROSSING THE INCHAVORE RIVER

A fortuitous arrangement of stones facilitates a none too easy crossing of the Inchavore River at the prominent copse of deciduous trees at 133046.

The terrain N of the copse is easy. S-wards towards Kanturk is more difficult. Just upstream of the copse a narrow path runs directly uphill S-ward through trees. This path is difficult to find if approaching the copse from the S. To do so, follow the firebreak E which runs along the upper side of the forest to the S of the copse, at its end taking the narrow path directly downhill (the clear firebreak shown on the current edition of sheet 56 does not exist).

ROUTE E12: CROSSING THE CLOGHOGE RIVER

There are stepping stones across the Cloghoge River at the two-storey house close to Lough Dan (152043) though they are difficult to cross unless the river is low.

WESTERN REGION

This region is bounded on the north by the section of the Sally Gap Road (R759) running west from Sally Gap, on the east by the Military Road (R115), on the south by the Wicklow Gap Road (R756) and on the west by Pollaphuca Reservoir.

General Access Problems

Because of the River Liffey, access southwards is impossible from the Sally Gap Road east of Ballysmuttan Bridge, for several miles to Coronation Plantation. Access is easier through the scattered trees of the Plantation and further south-east to Sally Gap. For the whole length of the Military Road from Sally Gap to Glenmacnass carpark (grid ref 1102) there are virtually no obstacles westward except for forest. The area south of this carpark is completely blocked by farmland. North of the Wicklow Gap Road extensive forest blocks access in many places. Though access is possible here and there, the only long clear stretch is from Wicklow Gap south-east for several miles. The road which runs along the eastern side of Pollaphuca Reservoir is blocked virtually everywhere by farmland, so the narrow road through open country from Lackan to Ballynultagh Gap and beyond to Ballysmuttan Bridge is most useful.

Terrain

We will begin with the line of hills overlooking the eastern shores of Pollaphuca Reservoir. Lugnagun, a shoulder rather than a peak, and Sorrel Hill are almost connected by a ditch traversing rough boggy ground. The summit of Sorrel has a distinctively large cairn on rock-strewn ground. Southwards is Ballynultagh Gap and beyond a long stretch of unforested, gently-sloping moorland runs to much steeper ground close to Mullaghcleevaun (849m), the second highest mountain in Wicklow. Standing at the apex of broad ridges to north-east, west and south it commands predictably good views, though with high rolling country in most directions, not as good as its elevation would suggest.

West of Mullaghcleevaun wet moorland extends to the subdued peaks of Moanbane (703m) and Silsean (698m) both of which command excellent views of the nearby Pollaphuca Reservoir as well as the plains of Kildare. North-east of Mullaghcleevaun to Sally Gap the backbone of the range runs over a line of unimpressive heathery peaks, including Duff Hill (720m) and Gravale (718m). Here an intermittent ditch running along the line of some of the summits is a useful aid in a difficult area for navigation. South of Mullaghcleevaun lies some very difficult ground, probably the most tiring in the entire range. Much of the high ground to Barnacullian consists of deep ravines and almost liquid bog, so it is far easier to make your way along the eastern edge rather than down the centre of the ridge.

South of Barnacullian the terrain improves: here lies the commanding peak of Tonelagee, the third highest in the range at 817m, with the great

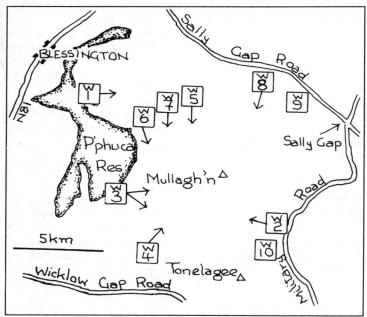

corrie containing Lough Ouler cut into its north-eastern flank. There is an easy approach to Tonelagee from the east on an attractive route overlooking Lough Ouler (though not as easy as a walk up from the Wicklow Gap!). South-east of the summit is a group of hills known collectively as the Brockaghs, whose summits are strewn with huge boulders, an unusual feature in this area.

ROUTE W1: NEAR LACKEN TO SORREL HILL

A forest walk ends on a shoulder offering good views of Pollaphuca Reservoir and much gently-sloped mountainside.

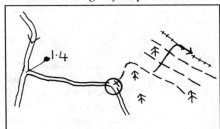

Approach: Turn L just after the Downshire Hotel in Blessington, shortly turn R to cross the bridge over the Reservoir (zero miles), turn R at the tee, turn L up a narrow laneway at 1.4 miles (signposted cul de sac). Park at the nearby forest entrance (003123).

Route: Take the track into forest to round a bend to the R. Turn L up the first wide grassy firebreak (it also carries an earthbank) to cross two forest tracks. On emerging from forest on the Lugnagun shoulder, turn R towards Sorrel to the E keeping forest initially on the R and later following a ditch.

ROUTE W2: MILITARY ROAD TO MULLAGHCLEEVAUN

An exceptionally high point (430m) begins a scenic, steadily uphill walk along practically the only rocky promontory in the area.

Approach: Drive to Sally Gap, continue straight ahead for over 5 miles to park in a tiny carpark on the R opposite a stand of old larches (101051). Note: If there are more than 2-3 cars in the party it is advisable to park in the forest entrance on the L a few hundred metres before reaching this carpark.

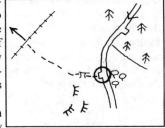

Route: Take the intermittent path from the carpark to keep to the R of the rocky promontory. Cross a nearby fence and eventually another at about 092058 on the way to Mullaghcleevaun East Top, an outlier of Mullaghcleevaun.

ROUTE W3: BALLYKNOCKAN TO MOANBANE, SILSEAN

The granite statues along the narrow roads here make this walk through Ballyknockan unusual, though the large quarry does not add to its attractions.

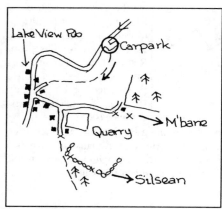

Approach: Turn L just after the Downshire Hotel in Blessington, shortly turn R to cross the bridge over the Reservoir, turn R at the tee and continue straight ahead to Ballyknockan (0070). If there are more than a few cars in the party it would be better to park in the carpark just before the village, as parking is limited in the village itself. If you park in the carpark take the narrow grassy track directly from the carpark into the village.

Route to Moanbane: With the Lake View pub on the R take the nearby second laneway on the L (or if coming from the carpark, take the first lane on the L in the village). Turn L at the nearby tee, continue past the quarry to the end of the road. Pass through two gates to keep forest on the L. Moanbane is directly E.

Route to Silsean: At the tee mentioned in the last paragraph, turn R and taking care not to mistakenly walk driveways, shortly cross a gate and take the track beyond. Where the stone wall on the L veers away from the track, walk through young trees to follow it. Cross the nearby second of two gates on the L, walk uphill through a field. Silsean lies to the E.

ROUTE W4: GLENBRIDE TO SILSEAN, MOANBANE, MULLAGHCLEEVAUN

A high starting point (370m) in a remote area leads through upland fields with wide but not spectacular views.

Approach: Take the N81 through <u>Blessington</u>, turn L onto the R758, drive through Valleymount, ignore the next turn on the L, but shortly after continue straight ahead where the R758 heads R. Ignore the junction R after about another mile, take the next turn L, drive to the bridge in Glenbride hamlet (037042).

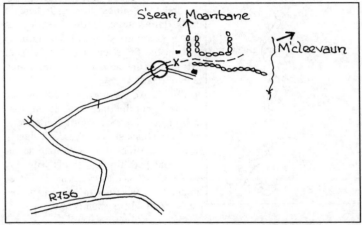

Route: From the bridge walk onward, forking immediately L to pass through a gate. For Silsean and Moanbane turn shortly L to pass between stone walls and reach open country with Silsean to the NW and Moanbane to the N. (Note: forest does not extend high onto Silsean as shown on the current edition of sheet 56.)

For Mullaghcleevaun pass through the gate mentioned in the last paragraph, walk onward along a rough track, and as you descend towards the Ballinagee River, veer away from fields on the R to cross the river. Mullaghcleevaun lies to the NE and Barnacullian to the E.

Note: If using this route for the return, look out for the track well above the fields that descend to the river.

ROUTE W5: NEAR BALLYNULTAGH GAP TO MULLAGH-CLEEVAUN

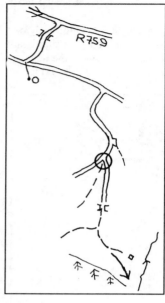

A short and what could be a pleasant stroll through upland fields, marred by long-standing 'temporary' dwellings and rubbish.

Approach: Take the N81 towards (not to) <u>Blessington</u>, turning L onto the R759. Follow the signs for Sally Gap for about 4.5 miles, turning R here to cross Ballysmuttan Bridge. Turn L at the tee (zero miles), ignore side turns to park in the forest entrance on the L at 2.1 miles (the second in a short distance) (058118).

Route: Take the narrow road running downhill (not the track to its R) to cross a bridge. Fork L shortly after and where the track starts to descend shortly to farm buildings, turn R to take an intermittent path through fields with forest some distance away on the R. Veer gradually to the river to avoid new forestry. Mullaghcleevaun is to the S.

ROUTE W6: BALLYNULTAGH GAP TO BLACK HILL

A simple walk from a high pass (450m) through open moorland with gradually expanding views.

Approach: Turn L just after the Downshire Hotel in <u>Blessington</u>, shortly turn R to cross the bridge over Pollaphuca Reservoir, turn R and continue straight ahead to Lackan (0111). Fork L here, drive about 2 miles to the carpark on the R (043108).

Route: Follow the bog road S which peters out in sub-roads near the summit of Black Hill. The sketch map is given with route W7.

Note: Sorrel Hill may also be easily climbed from Ballynultagh Gap, though there is no path.

ROUTE W7: BALLYNULTAGH GAP TO MULLAGHCLEEVAUN

From a high starting point (450m), a walk which is nearly all on grassy track flanked by scattered trees, and ends near a col between Black Hill and Mullaghcleevaun.

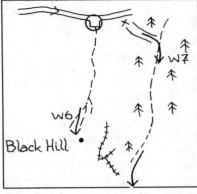

Approach: Turn L just after the Downshire Hotel in <u>Blessington</u>, shortly turn R to cross the bridge over Pollaphuca Reservoir, turn R and continue straight ahead to Lackan (0111). Fork L here, drive about 2 miles to the carpark on the R (043108). It is also possible to park on the roadside a little further on.

Route: Walk the road onward (NE) from the carpark to cross the first gate on the R after about 5 mins. Walk downhill through a grassy gap in the forest to reach a wide forestry track. Turn R onto it, follow it to its end and continue generally S on a rough, wet path which peters out close to a fence junction near the col at about 0408, from which Mullaghcleevaun is about 3km away to the SE.

ROUTE W8: SALLY GAP ROAD TO GRAVALE

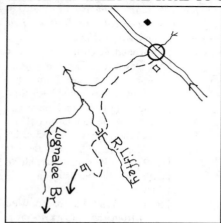

An initially pleasant approach to Gravale through the scattered trees of the Coronation Plantation, beyond which lies extensive moorland.

Approach: Turn R (NE) at <u>Sally Gap</u>, drive for less than 3 miles to park near a derelict house on the L or a house on the R beyond it (097134).   Parking is difficult hereabouts. This point may also be conveniently reached from the W.

Route: Take the track just to the W of the derelict house, cross the River Liffey on a bridge, then either walk upwards along the track to another derelict house or along the bank of the Lugnalee Brook. Gravale lies to the S.

ROUTE W9: CROSSING THE RIVER LIFFEY

The River Liffey and a nearby tributary may be crossed from the Sally Gap Road, thus allowing access to Gravale and Duff Hill.

Approach: Turn R (NE) at <u>Sally Gap</u>, drive for less than 2 miles to park on waste ground on the L just beyond a bridge (109128).

Route: Walk about 100m downstream, cross the two rivers on iron girders.

ROUTE W10: CROSSING THE GLENMACNASS RIVER

The Glenmacnass River may be crossed on stepping stones about 70m upstream from the large carpark on the <u>Military Road</u> at Glenmacnass (113029). This allows easy access to Tonelagee and Stoney Top. Alternatively, there is a bridge over 1km upstream from the carpark.

SOUTH-EAST REGION

This region is bounded to the north by the Wicklow Gap Road (R756) east of the Gap; and to the west by the main watershed, that is from Wicklow Gap, through Turlough Hill to Table and Lugnaquillia.

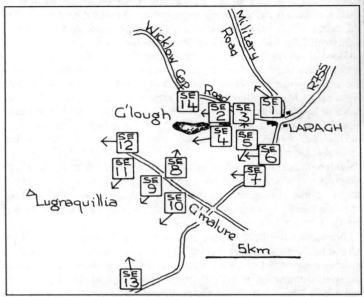

General Access Difficulties

This region is fairly difficult to access from the Wicklow Gap Road south because of forest and the Glendasan River, which is difficult (but not impossible) to ford. From Glendalough access in all directions is easy, except where the way is barred by steep ground. Access from Glenmalure south-westwards is difficult because of farmland and the Avonbeg River. It is a little easier north-eastwards despite forestry and steep ground.

South of Glenmalure the Military Road traverses a spur of high ground to reach Aughavannagh. Croaghanmoira to its east is easily reached from the top of the pass between Glenmalure and Aughavannagh but forest effectively blocks the way to the Lugnaquillia massif to the west.

41

Terrain

The most northerly spur in the region lies between Glendalough and Glendasan, a small valley scarred by mine workings. At its easterly end is twin-topped Camaderry (698m), which gives easy walking. Unfortunately, directly to its west is Turlough Hill Reservoir, an unwelcome intrusion in an otherwise unspoilt environment. Further west is some of the most difficult terrain in Wicklow, consisting of a rolling bogland with only small lakes and Art's Cross (038990) as landmarks.

Glendalough itself is a highly scenic and historic valley, though it attracts a large number of day trippers in summer. The mountains around are generally most attractive. Derrybawn (474m) boasts an ancient oakwood on its lower northerly slopes. From it a fine, narrow rocky ridge leads to less than impressive Mullacor (657m). Due south of the Upper Lake is the Spink, a scenic ridge leading to the attractive Lugduff ridge (652m), and further west into boggy ground around Conavalla (734m) and Table (701m).

South of the entire area described in the last paragraph is the deep, narrow valley of Glenmalure, more remote than Glendalough and nearly as scenic. South of it again rises the highest ground in Wicklow, the Lugnaquillia massif. Though split between this section and the next we will briefly describe the entire massif here.

Lugnaquillia itself (925m) has a modest, grassy summit. To compensate it has two spectacular corries, the North and South Prisons, cut into its otherwise bland form. This summit is the centre of a series of radiating spurs culminating in modestly rising peaks, separated by high valleys and scenic lakes. Starting at the north and working clockwise we will now briefly describe these spurs.

Directly north of Lugnaquillia a useful path runs along high ground to Camenabologue (758m). East of this spur is the Fraughan Rock Glen, one of the remotest and loveliest valleys in the entire mountain area. The spur running east from Lugnaquillia splits to enclose scenic Kelly's Lough, one sub-spur culminating in Cloghernagh (600m), the other in Carrawaystick and Corrigasleggaun (794m). The spurs to the south of Lugnaquillia are more modest, and mostly clothed in forest, though the remote valley of the Ow River is highly attractive. To the west of Lugnaquillia a divided spur runs over Slievemaan (759m) to the south-west and Camara Hill (480m) to the west, both spurs offering easy walking over short grass.

42

ROUTE SE1: LARAGH TO BROCKAGHS

Mature forest with pleasant views to reach open country on the slopes of the Brockaghs.

Approach: Drive to <u>Laragh</u>, cross the main bridge in the village, turn immediately R, turn R at McCoy's shop, park carefully at the forest entrance a little way up (139968). Bus: St Kevin's.

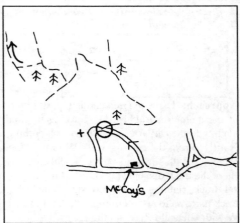

Route: Take the forest track to walk around a hairpin bend, ignore a track on the R to continue uphill, walk round a hairpin bend to the L and then turn R uphill.

Where thick forest shortly ceases on the L (at a right-angle bend to the R in the track) turn L uphill on a rough path to reach open country with the high ground of the Brockaghs reaching roughly NW.

Note 1: This route is difficult to find if walking in the opposite direction. However, there are at least two prominent notices around grid ref 1397 that are close to forest on the spur S of the Brockaghs and are located at points where tracks lead down through the forest to Laragh.

Note 2: Although this route starts in the South-East region it leads into the mountains of the West region.

Note 3: The NPWS 1:25 000 map available at the Glendalough Centre is particularly helpful in this area.

ROUTE SE2: GLENDALOUGH TO GLENEALO

From the valley of Glenealo it is possible to climb to any of the peaks from Lugduff round to Camaderry. A track or path to start and then a pathless gentle slope with a stream alongside into lovely, remote terrain W of Glendalough.

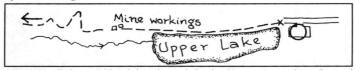

Approach: Drive to <u>Glendalough</u>, park in the Upper Carpark at the end of the motor road (111964). Parking is prohibited on the narrow road leading to the carpark, where there is a parking charge. Bus: St Kevin's.

Route: From the carpark walk W to the Upper Lake (there are several routes). With the lake on the L, take the track to the mine workings (here the track disappears). Beyond these a clear path graduates to a zig-zag track, running moderately steeply uphill and still generally W. The track narrows to an intermittent path on more level ground and continues W with Glenealo River on the L.

ROUTE SE3: GLENDALOUGH TO CAMADERRY

Good views over Glendalough to start, even better views later on, on a steep path which climbs directly from Glendalough into open ground on the side of Camaderry.

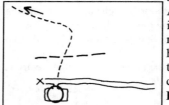

Approach: Drive to <u>Glendalough</u>, park in the Upper Carpark at the end of the motor road (111964). Parking is prohibited on the narrow road leading to the carpark, where there is a parking charge. Bus: St Kevin's.

Route: Climb steeply upward on the path on the opposite side of the road. Cross a forest track and continue upwards. The path eventually bends L and continues nearly all the way to the SE top of Camaderry (677m).

Note: If you want to avoid the steep ascent, walk a short distance along the shore of the Upper Lake, turn acutely R onto a track at a derelict house. Continue on this track NE and then W to reach the E side of Camaderry. This is a much longer route.

ROUTE SE4: GLENDALOUGH TO LUGDUFFS

Rapids and pleasant mature forest near at hand to start, then a stiff climb to the Lugduff Spink, with lovely views in all directions.

Approach: Drive to Glendalough, park in the Upper Carpark at the end of the motor road (111964). Parking is prohibited on the narrow road leading to the carpark, where there is a parking charge. Bus: St Kevin's.

Route: Walk S from the carpark across open ground, cross the bridge at the foot of steep ground ahead, climb the path with Pollanass Waterfall on the L to join a forest track. Continue upward to turn first R onto another forest track. At the first hairpin bend, a L, cross the stile on the R. Climb W through young trees to reach mature trees and then climb steeply beside them to the crest of the hill ahead. On open ground with forest on the L and cliffs on the R, follow a clear, muddy path W. After about 2km it graduates to a track climbing SW towards the Lugduffs.

Note 1: The path along the Spink is badly eroded. Use this area only when necessary and take great care to minimise further damage. See also the Country Code (p.10).

Note 2: Coming from the other direction watch out carefully for the path L off the crest of the Spink.

ROUTE SE5: GLENDALOUGH TO DERRYBAWN

A lovely uphill walk on tracks through mature forest is followed by a steep, clear path leading directly to open ground close to the summit of Derrybawn.

Approach: Drive to Glendalough, park in the Upper Carpark at the end of the motor road (111964). Parking is prohibited on the narrow road leading to the carpark, where there is a parking charge. Bus: St Kevin's.

Route: Walk S from the carpark across open ground, cross the bridge at the foot of steep ground ahead, climb the path with Pollanass Waterfall on the L to join a forest track. Continue upward on the track to turn first L and cross two nearby bridges. Ignore a nearby minor fork L. At the pillar on the L just be- 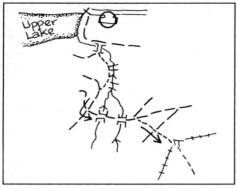 yond it turn R to follow a rough path uphill and cross another forest track. Continue upwards to reach open ground at a stile at 114956 with a path leading to Derrybawn nearby to the E.

ROUTE SE6: MILITARY ROAD TO DERRYBAWN

Varied terrain of fields and mature forest to start, then an upland track with open ground on one side along the shoulder of Derrybawn.

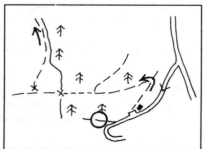

Approach: Take the R755 from <u>Laragh</u>, turning R towards Glenmalure about 1 mile S (zero miles). At 0.6 miles, pass a track on the R and take the nearby next track on this side. Park on waste ground on the L after about 100m (133947). There is only limited parking hereabouts. Bus: St Kevin's.

Route: Walk back to tarmac, turn L and take the nearby first track on the L. Turn first L sharply back, continue straight ahead to the first hairpin bend, a R. Turn L off the track here to pass through a gate visible from the track. Now in open terrain, cross the first gate R onto another track. Continue gently upward to the crest of the spur. Just over the crest take a rough path on the L heading W for Derrybawn.

46

ROUTE SE7: MILITARY ROAD TO CULLENTRAGH, MULLACOR

A high start (370m) gives a gentle uphill stroll through coniferous trees in various stages of growth, with good but not spectacular views.

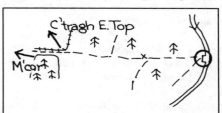

Approach: Drive to <u>Laragh</u>, continue S on the R755 for about 1 mile to turn R towards Glenmalure. Park after about 3 miles at the forest entrance on the R just beyond the crest of the hill or in the carpark just before it (131923).

Route: Ignore the major track L at the forest entrance to walk straight ahead, cross a gate R to continue in the same direction, ignore a minor turn R. Cross at the fence corner after about 20 mins from the start to climb to the nearby E summit of Cullentragh (over 460m). For Mullacor do not cross the fence. Instead continue straight ahead on a path to the nearby band of mature forest. From here Mullacor and the main summit of Cullentragh lie to the W.

ROUTE SE8: GLENMALURE TO MULLACOR

A lovely path giving excellent views down into Glenmalure is followed by a forest track offering equally good views, though the scenery close at hand is not so good.

Approach: Turn R at <u>Drumgoff crossroads</u> (zero miles). At 2.0 miles park in the forest carpark on the R (082927).

Route: Take the path from the corner of the carpark across a bridge and climb to a forest track. Turn L here, walk round a hairpin bend to meet the Wicklow Way, whose present (1997) route is followed from here on. Turn L onto a path, take it upwards to another forest track. Turn R here and sharply L at the next junction. Fork R at the next junction and L at the tee. After 5 mins walking from here turn R onto a muddy path which emerges from forest at about 087936, with Mullacor close to the E and the saddle between it and the Lugduff ridge to the NW.

ROUTE SE9 : GLENMALURE TO ART'S LOUGH

A gently rising forest track offers good views over Glenmalure and beyond. At its end, a rough path through heather ends at Art's Lough, a dramatic location high on the Lugnaquillia massif.

Approach: Turn R at <u>Drumgoff crossroads</u> (zero miles). At 2.0 miles park in the forest carpark on the R (082927). You can also park a little

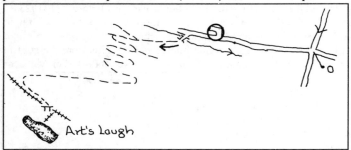

further on at the bridge on the L.

Route: Walk onward (NW) along the road, turn L shortly to cross a bridge. Ignoring minor branches, continue upward on a track to its end, here taking a rough path which shortly bends L uphill to run parallel to a fence. Cross this fence on a stile at Art's Lough.

Note: The track mentioned above runs to within a few hundred metres of the E of Art's Lough, much higher than shown on the current edition of sheet 56.

ROUTE SE10: GLENMALURE TO CLOHERNAGH

A sometimes wet track, offering lovely views over Glenmalure and beyond, ends on high ground, with Kelly's Lough and several peaks including Clohernagh within easy reach.

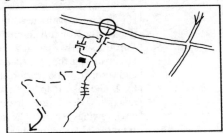

Approach: Turn R at <u>Drumgoff crossroads</u> (zero miles), park on the verge at 1.4 miles with a track and a cottage backed by trees on the L (088921). Park is limited, so please do so carefully.

Route: Walk the track to cross a bridge ahead, ford a nearby stream on stepping stones, walk round the L of the cottage and take the rough track beyond into open country. Keep to the track which zig-zags upwards to peter out at about 080919, with Clohernagh to the W.

Note 1: Please do not disturb the residents in the cottage. In particular there may be notices indicating another route to that given here. If so, obey them.

Note 2: The above track is shown correctly on sheet 56, but other tracks shown on this map to the N and S of Carrawaystick Brook do not exist.

ROUTE SE11: GLENMALURE TO LUGNAQUILLIA

The reward for a dull purgatorial forest track to start is the heavenly, dramatic terrain of the Fraughan Rock Glen.

Approach: Turn R at <u>Drumgoff crossroads</u> to park in Baravore carpark about 3 miles on at the head of the valley (067942).

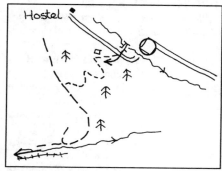

Route: Take a path upstream to cross the river by a nearby footbridge. Cross the road and directly opposite take a grassy track (farther on a path) heading diagonally R uphill through forest, shortly passing a large ruin on the R. At its end turn L onto a forest track and take it to its first junction where the main track swings sharply R, a minor track continues straight ahead and a stream is close by on the L. Cross the stream (it may be difficult after rain) and, keeping between a fence and the stream to avoid private property, walk upward to the foot of a cascade at about 049934. Lugnaquillia lies to the SW.

Note: If walking downhill, pass a shelter belt of trees on the R and cross the stream just after (you will clearly see the forest track beyond the stream). Keep to this track (rather than trying to find the path mentioned above) and turn R at the youth hostel.

ROUTE SE12: GLENMALURE TO TABLE, CAMENABOLOGUE
Forest to start and then a gradually deteriorating track in open country (though with forestry near at hand) to end at a high pass.

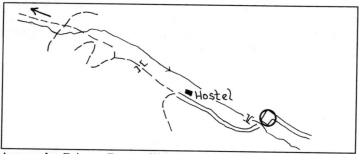

Approach: Drive to <u>Drumgoff crossroads</u>, turn R and park in the large carpark at Baravore about 3 miles further on (067942).

50

Route: Cross the stream a few metres upstream on a footbridge. Walk the tarmac road beyond to the youth hostel, ignore the forest track on the L here to continue straight ahead. (The route from here is generally NW following the old track to the pass at 0296. The following details are given purely for reassurance.) Cross a wooden bridge, shortly turn R at a tee, ignore a U-turn in the new forest track on the L, ford a stream shortly. Cross a forestry track and continue straight ahead to the pass between Table to the N and Camenabologue to the S.

ROUTE SE13: AUGHAVANNAGH TO LUG, CARRAWAYSTICK

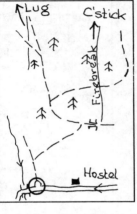

Much forest track to negotiate on a long, not too attractive route which nonetheless gives the easiest approach to Lugnaquillia from the S.

Approach: Drive ahead at <u>Drumgoff crossroads</u> for 5 miles, turn R here to pass the youth hostel, park shortly at the forest entrance on the R (056861).

Route to Lugnaquillia: Take the forest track, fork first R, turn L at the tee (where there is a prominent bridge to the R). Ignoring shortly a track on the R, walk steadily uphill for about 2km, here forking R. Emerge from forest at about 036905, with Lugnaquil-

lia to N, reached by diverting L of the direct approach to avoid the South Prison. Note: The point at which you enter forest is clearly visible when walking downhill.

Route to Carrawaystick: At the prominent bridge, climb the wide firebreak to cross a track, continue N until out of trees on the S spur of Carrawaystick. Note: As this route is difficult to find on the way down, head instead for the forest track on the E of the S spur of Carrawaystick.

ROUTE SE14: CROSSING THE GLENMACNASS RIVER

The river may usually be forded from a layby (098985) 1.9 miles from the Glendalough end of the Wicklow Gap Road. Camaderry is to the SW.

SOUTH-WEST REGION

This region comprises the area bounded on the north by the section of the Wicklow Gap Road (R756) west of the Gap; and to the west of the main watershed, that is from Wicklow Gap, through Turlough Hill to Table and Lugnaquillia southwards.

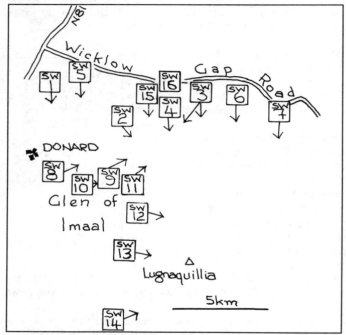

General Access Difficulties

It is comparatively difficult to access the mountains south of the Wicklow Gap Road because of forest and the unfordable King's River, so the few minor roads leading south off the Wicklow Gap Road are useful. It is also difficult to access from the west because of farming land and further south the Glen of Imaal Artillery Range, though there are established routes along the perimeter of the range.

Terrain

The area south of the Wicklow Gap Road in this region is navigationally some of the toughest in Wicklow, consisting of a rolling bogland with only small lakes as landmarks. The spurs reaching north from this bogland towards the Wicklow Gap Road are equally featureless and difficult to navigate over. Though there are only two lakes at Three Lakes (0398), Art's Cross (038990), which actually is a vertical crucifix, is therefore a useful landmark in this area.

The western side of the region is dominated by the broad basin of the Glen of Imaal, much of which is an artillery range and mostly off-limits, though there are two routes waymarked by the Army through its periphery. To the north is a group of modest, gently-sloped summits of which the most distinctive is Church (544m). Much of the lower slopes of the undistinguished mountainside south of Church to Lobawn is forested. From Lobawn east towards Table Mountain, a scenic area with wide views especially good over the Glen and towards the Lugnaquillia massif, a series of pillars and a ditch are useful aids to navigation.

The mountains to the east of the Glen of Imaal have already been briefly dealt with in the South-East region. South of the Glen, Keadeen (653m) is a fairly attractive peak looking out onto the plains of Kildare and beyond. However it is really an outlier and not part of the main range.

ROUTE SW1:   NEAR HOLLYWOOD TO CHURCH MOUNTAIN

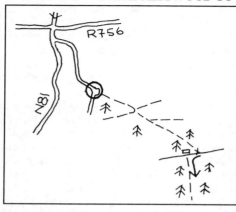

A pleasant walk on track through forest is followed by a steady ascent along a wide firebreak to the upper slopes of Church.

Approach: Drive through <u>Blessington</u>, pass the junction of the R756 and shortly take the next turn L. Drive onward for 1.1 miles to the forest entrance on the L (937033), where there is space for several cars.

Route: Walk the forest track to the nearby first hairpin bend, a R. Here take a gently climbing minor track. Ignoring an even more minor track L, continue to a narrow band of mature forest. Cross the gate at its end, turn R to a nearby ruin and walk directly upward from here, mature trees on the R, lower trees on the L. Passing a turning circle on the L continue directly upward to reach open ground near the summit.

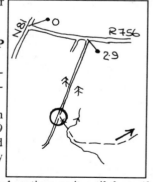

ROUTE SW2:   OFF WICKLOW GAP ROAD TO ROUND HILL

A track leads through rough, gently-sloped lowland bog into rough, gently-sloped upland bog.

Approach: Drive through <u>Blessington</u>, turn L onto the R756 (zero miles), turn R at 2.9 miles (the second of two closely spaced junctions). At 5.1 miles park at the gateway on the L with a track beyond (980004).

Route: Take the track to cross a stream and continue on it until the track peters out after 1.5km or so. Round Hill lies to the E.

ROUTE SW3: WICKLOW GAP ROAD TO OAKWOOD, LOUGH FIRRIB

A wide forest track running gently uphill, then a muddy track through a clear-felled area into forest. The route ends in remote country N of the Oakwood spur.

Approach: Drive through <u>Blessington</u>, turn L off the N81 onto the R756. Drive for 7.3 miles to cross the prominent Ballinagee Bridge. Turn R onto the nearby first track to park around a bridge (033020).

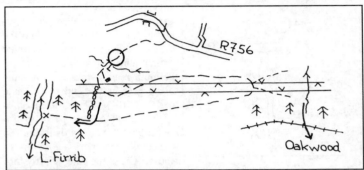

Route for Oakwood: Cross the bridge, take the R fork shortly after (the L ends at a house). Follow the track as it swings L under power lines and continue gently uphill to where the track swings R in a wide hairpin bend with the power lines again overhead. Turn L off the track here onto a gently rising path (not the descending path just before it) which soon peters out in forest. Contour for a few minutes more through forest to reach young trees beyond a stream. Turn R to walk upstream and emerge into open country at 042009 with the Oakwood spur to the S.

Route for Lough Firrib: Instead of following the track where it swings L, continue upward through rough vegetation into forest following a stone wall. Turn R onto the first track, walk to open country at Glenreemore Brook (023010), turn L upstream to follow the Brook to its source. Lough Firrib is to the S.

Note 1: It is virtually impossible to follow the Oakwood route if walking downhill. Instead take the wide firebreak on the E bank of the lower reaches of Glenreemore Brook (not shown on the current edition of sheet 56) and turn R onto the first track to reach the start of this route.

Note 2: Route SW4 describes another, easier way of reaching Glenreemore Brook.

ROUTE SW4: OFF WICKLOW GAP ROAD TO LOUGH FIRRIB

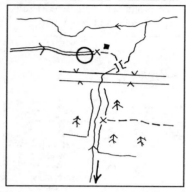

A wide gap in forest alongside a stream ends in remote, open country N of Lough Firrib.

Approach: Drive through <u>Blessington</u>, turn L off the N81 onto the R756. After 3 miles, continue straight ahead on a side road where the main road swings L. Continue to the gate at the end of the side road (022014). (This side road is 3.7 miles long and becomes increasingly rutted towards its end, so it is advisable to park before this.)

Route: Cross the gate, shortly turn R over a bridge, walk upwards through a wide firebreak with Glenreemore Brook on the R to cross the end of a forest track. Continue upstream to its source. Lough Firrib lies to the S.

Note 1: The wide firebreak on the E bank of the lower reaches of Glenreemore Brook is not shown on the current edition of sheet 56.

Note 2: If coming in the opposite direction this firebreak is clearly visible.

ROUTE SW5: WICKLOW GAP ROAD TO CORRIEBRACKS

A simple route on narrow road and track leads to near the summit of one of the most undistinguished of Wicklow's mountains.

Approach: Drive through <u>Blessington</u>, turn R onto the R756 (zero miles). Park at the minor road R at 2.7 miles (967037). Parking is possible but difficult on the Wicklow Gap Road. A few cars might be parked at the end of tarmac 0.7 miles along the minor road.

Route: Walk to the end of the minor road and continue on a narrow track upward to its end just N of Corriebracks.

ROUTE SW6: WICKLOW GAP ROAD TO FAIR MOUNTAIN

A pleasant gently-sloped walk along stream banks with at best only a wet intermittent path to reach a remote valley close to Fair Mountain.

Approach: Drive to <u>Glendalough</u>, fork R onto the R756 to reach Wicklow Gap (zero miles), park at 1.2 miles at Glashaboy Bridge (065017). This point may also be reached from the W.

Route: Follow the river downstream and, keeping close to it enter forest. Pass under two sets of power lines running through open ground, cross a narrow but deep tributary and continue generally downhill to follow the

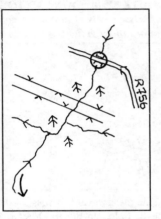

main stream round a right angle bend to the R. Just beyond this bend walk upstream along a major tributary flowing here NE and so reach a minor valley 1km W of the summit of Fair Mountain.

ROUTE SW7: WICKLOW GAP ROAD TO TURLOUGH HILL
Tarmac all the way to a high point (660m) close to Camaderry.
Approach: Drive to <u>Glendalough</u>, fork R onto the R756, park in the carpark at the Wicklow Gap (076002). This is at the second of two nearby tarmac roads on the L. (Note: cars are not allowed on the road to the Upper Reservoir.) This point may also be easily reached from the W.
Route: Follow the tarmac road generally S (there are also one or two places where rough paths can be used to cut U-turns) to reach high ground close to the Upper Reservoir, with Camaderry close to the E and Lough Firrib to the W.

ROUTE SW8: DONARD TO LOBAWN
A pleasant walk on a narrow country lane is followed by a track gently upward through fields with long but only gradually unfolding views.

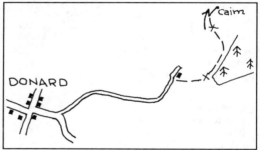

Approach: Park in <u>Donard</u>.
Route: Take the road towards Ballinclea youth hostel, turning first L, signposted Kilcoagh. After 1.5km, where the road terminates at a farmhouse, take a track on the R just inside the farmyard. Cross a gate L to keep on the track, forest now on the R, fields on the L. Veer L with the track to pass through another gate. Continue on the track to reach a large cairn on the W spur of Lobawn, from where a fence and later an intermittent ditch runs to the summit.

ROUTE SW9: SNUGBOROUGH BRIDGE TO LOBAWN
A walk through varied terrain is spoilt by litter and untidiness near farmhouses. The alternative route partly avoids this disfigurement.
Approach: From <u>Donard</u> (zero miles) take the road towards (not to) Ballinclea youth hostel. After 1.4 miles cross Snugborough Bridge and

park around the track on the L immediately after (951964) or along the track itself.

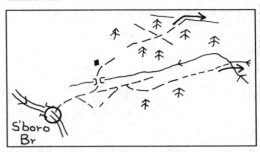

Route: Walk the track, ignore two minor tracks R, cross a bridge (the alternative route - see below - starts just before this bridge). Keep on the track past a farmhouse and continue straight ahead to the track's end in a field, from where the resumed track can be seen entering forest ahead. Take this to cross another track and so reach open ground at about 960977. Lobawn is in line with the forest edge to the E.

Alternative: Just before the bridge, take a minor track on the R, ignore an acute track on the R, fork shortly R uphill and continue through scattered trees to the track's end. Continue on an intermittent path to reach open country at 968974 with Lobawn to the NE and Sugarloaf to the S.

Note: In the opposite direction it is easy to find the alternative route by aiming for the steep river valleys at about 9697 and taking the path into scattered trees just S of the rivers' confluence.

ROUTE SW 10: NEAR DONARD TO LOBAWN

A comparatively high start on a track running mostly through forest ends on the shoulder of Lobawn.

Approach: Drive to <u>Donard</u>, take the road towards Ballinclea youth hostel for 0.7 miles, park in the forest entrance on the L.

Route: Walk the forest track to a fork reached in about 20 mins. Take the (minor) L fork to meet open country at a gate near a forest corner at 959976 with Lobawn to the E.

ROUTE SW11: NEAR SNUGBOROUGH BRIDGE TO SUGARLOAF

A normally extremely muddy track through forest ends with good views from the SW slopes of Sugarloaf over the Glen of Imaal.

Approach: From <u>Donard</u> (zero miles) take the road towards (not to) Ballinclea youth hostel. Cross Snugborough Bridge (1.4 miles), park at the wide forest entrance on the L at 2.1 miles (954956).

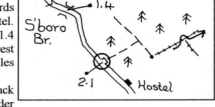

Route: Follow the forest track to a tee (there is a large boulder in the centre of the track to the R). Turn R to reach the end of the track in about 5 mins. Turn L uphill here to ascend by the edge of a field, forest on the L. At the top of the field, avoid a fence ahead by veering briefly into forest. Sugarloaf lies to the N.

ROUTE SW12: KNICKEEN TO TABLE, CAMENABOLOGUE

Mature forest allows good views to the Lugnaquillia massif. There is little climbing until a short, sharp ascent at the end.

Approach: From <u>Donard</u> drive past Ballinclea youth hostel (zero miles) and continue straight ahead where the main road turns R. At 1.7 miles park at the forest entrance on the L (982948).

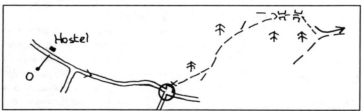

Route: (Note: the route is indicated by waymarks.) Cross the gate into forest and continue straight ahead for 3km (about 30 mins). At a hairpin bend L turn R off the track to cross two nearby wooden bridges. Climb with a clear-felled area close on the R. At its end turn L onto a wide track. Keep on it to the pass between Table and Camenabologue.

ROUTE SW13: NEAR FENTON'S TO CAMARA HILL

An easy ascent to Camara Hill with gradually widening views, which are particularly good to the N. Camara Hill affords the easiest approach to Lugnaquillia.

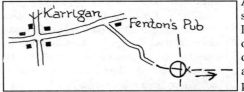

Approach: The route starts at a tee at 984929. It should be approached only from the W as the other roads are impassable to cars, and the potholes on this one demand caution. Take the road from <u>Donard</u> past Ballinclea youth hostel, turning shortly first R and L at Knockanarrigan (signposted). Turn R onto a narrow road just before Fenton's Pub 1.0 miles further on (it might be advisable to park here). Drive 0.8 miles to the tee, where there is ample parking.

Route: Take the track E uphill, indicated by Army waymarks. Shortly narrowing to a path, it keeps to the crest of the spur to Camara Hill and beyond it towards Lugnaquillia.

ROUTE SW14: BALLINFOYLE TO BALLINEDDAN

After an convoluted car journey a short and simple route on track from a high point (310m) on a minor road through low trees to reach open country with Ballineddan ahead.

Approach: From <u>Donard</u> drive past Ballinclea youth hostel, turning R just beyond it for Knockanarrigan (zero miles). Continue straight ahead here, veer R over a bridge after 0.5 miles and turn L immediately. Fork L at 2.4 miles, and park at the junction at 3.0 miles (986902).

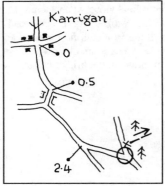

Route: Take the L (N) fork at the junction, shortly cross a gate on the R and walk upwards along a firebreak. Cross another gate to reach open country with Ballineddan and Slievemaan to the E.

ROUTE SW 15: OFF WICKLOW GAP ROAD TO ROUND HILL

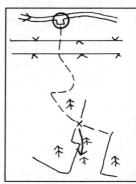

A forest track ends with a walk upward through young trees, ending on high ground close to the spur called Round Hill (511m).

Approach: Drive through <u>Blessington,</u> turn L off the N81 onto the R756. After 3 miles, continue straight ahead on a side road where the main road swings L. Continue for 2.4 miles to a forest entrance on the R (001014).

Route: Take the forest track upwards to pass under power lines. Further up cross a gate beyond which the track levels out and there are young trees on both sides. Turn R off the track here and walk carefully through the trees to reach open ground close to the cairn marking the summit of Round Hill.

Note: if coming in the opposite direction watch out for 2 blocks of forest a few hundred metres apart and walk down the E side of the W block.

ROUTE SW16:   CROSSING THE KING'S RIVER

The footbridge (at 003016) near Granabeg allows access from the Wicklow Gap Road to the mountains to the S.   It is not shown on the maps.

Route: Start at the old schoolhouse in Granabeg (0002), which is on the S of the road directly opposite a junction.   Take the path just to the R of the schoolhouse when facing it.   Walk down through fields to cross the bridge, walk to the nearby road.   From the other direction: if you are walking W along the minor road running parallel to, and S of the King's River cross a small bridge, pass through a gate on the R immediately (from where the bridge is barely visible).

LIST OF PRINCIPAL PEAKS

Each peak's name is followed by its grid reference (with the 1:50 000 map on which it features if not sheet 56), its height, the identifying features on its summit (except cairns unless unusual in some way), and the access routes leading to it. Indistinct peaks are indicated by an asterisk (*).

Ballineddan 0090, 652m, SW13

*Ballymorefinn Hill 0820 (50), 525m, N9

Barnacullian 0704, 714m, metal post

Ben Leagh 0394, 689m, SE11

Black Hill 0409, 602m, W6

Brockagh (highest) 1099, 557m, SE1

Camaderry NW 0898, 698m, SE2 SE3 SE14 SW7

Camara Hill 9992, 480m, SW13

Camenabologue 0296, 758m, SE12, SW12

*Carrawaystick 0790, 597m, SE13

Carrig 9588 (62), 571m

Carrigshouk 0905, 571m

Carrigvoher 1210, 682m, large boulders W9

Church Mountain 9401, 544m, heaps of stones, SW1

Clohernagh 0591, 800m, SE9 SE10

Conavalla 0397, 734m, post

Corriebracks 9600, 531m, SW5

Corrig 0919, 618m, small pillar, N11

*Corrigasleggaun 0491, 794m

Croaghanmoira Mtn, 0986 (62), 664m, trig pillar

Croghan Mtn, 1372 (62), 606m, trig pillar

Cruagh, 1321 (50), about 520m, N13 N2

Cullentragh 1193, 510m, SE7

Derrybawn 1195, 474m, SE5 SE6

Djouce 1710, 725m, trig pillar, E4 E6 E9 E10

Duff Hill 0908, 720m, boulder field

Fair Mountain 0600, 569m, large boulders, SW6

Fairy Castle 1722 (50), 536m, N1 N3 N4

Fananierin, 1189 (62), 426m

Fancy 1507, 595m, E8

Gravale 1009, 718m, boulder field, W8 W9

Kanturk 1203, 523m, E7 E11

Keadeen 9589, 653m (62), trig pillar

Kilmashogue 1523 (50), 408m

Kippure 1115, 757m, TV mast, N6 N8 N12

Knocknacloghoge 1405, 534m, E8 E7

*Knocknagun 1618, 555m, prominent tor, N10

63

Lobawn 9797, 636m, small pillar, SW8 SW9 SW10

Lugduff (highest) 0795, 652m, white quartzite rocks, SE2 SE4 SE8

Lugnaquillia 0391, 925m, trig pillar, SE9 SE11 SE13 SW13

*Lybagh 0289 (62), 646m

Maulin 1813, 570m, E4 E2

Moanbane 0306, 703m, W3 W4

Mullacor 0993, 657m, SE4 SE7 SE8

Mullaghcleevaun 0607, 849m, trig pillar, W2 W4 W5 W7

Mullaghcleevaun East Top 0806, over 790m, W2

*Oakwood 0499, 619m, SW3

Prince William's Seat 1718, 555m, trig pillar, N5 N7 N10

*Round Hill, 0099, 511m, SW2 SW15

Scarr 1301, 641m, E3 E5

Seahan 0819, 648m, megalithic tomb, N14 N9

Seefin 0716, 621m, megalithic tomb N15

Seefingan 0816, 724m, megalithic tomb N15

Silsean 0205, 698m, small lakes, W3 W4

Slievemaan 0190, 759m, SW14

Sorrel Hill 0411, 599m, large cairn, W1

Stoney Top 0802, 714m

Sugarloaf 9696, 552m, SW11

*Table 0197, 701m, SE12 SW12

Three Rock 1723 (50), over 440m, prominent tors, N1

Tibradden 1425 (50), 467m, passage grave, N3

Tonduffs 1513, 642m, E1

Tonelagee 0801, 817m, trig pillar, W10

War Hill 1611, 686m

*White Hill 1708, 630m, E6 E10

SYMBOLS

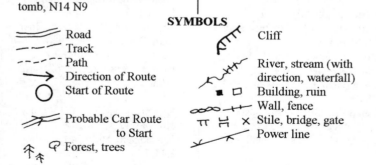

Road
Track
Path
Direction of Route
Start of Route

Probable Car Route to Start

Forest, trees

Cliff

River, stream (with direction, waterfall)

Building, ruin

Wall, fence

Stile, bridge, gate

Power line